*A Sunset Pictorial*

# Beautiful Hawaii

Lane Publishing Co., Menlo Park, California

# Edited by Dorothy Krell

Design: **JoAnn Masaoka**

Maps and Illustrations: **Dick Cole**

Front cover: Kona Coast, Hawaii. Back cover:
Kalalau Valley, Kauai. Photographs by David Muench.

Editor, Sunset Books: David E. Clark

Seventh printing November 1985

This book was printed and bound by Kingsport Press, Kingsport, Tennessee, from litho film prepared by Graphic Arts Center, Portland, Oregon. Body type is Optima; type for heads is Friz Quadrata, composed by Paul O. Giesey, Adcrafters, Portland, Oregon. Paper for pages is Velvo Enamel made by Westvaco Corp., Luke, Maryland.

# Beautiful Hawaii

# Contents

Kauai

Niihau

oLihue

Oahu

Honolulu
o

# An Introduction to
# Beautiful Hawaii

Some 25 million years ago, molten lava began to bubble up out of a fissure at the bottom of the sea. This was the beginning of the Hawaiian Ridge, the great range of volcanic mountains that today stretches for 1,600 miles across the Pacific Ocean just below the Tropic of Cancer. From ocean depths of more than 15,000 feet, the highest peaks rise above the surface of the sea to form the islands, islets, and atolls of the Hawaiian chain. Measured from the ocean floor, Mauna Kea on the island of Hawaii is the tallest mountain in the world, rising 13,796 feet above sea level and extending 19,680 feet below—a total of 33,476 feet.

Now once-bare lava slopes support gardens that blaze with bougainvillea, anthuriums, bird-of-paradise plants, orchids, hibiscus, and plumeria. Cattle range over cool grasslands below mountain summits that are tipped with snow in winter. Waterfalls spill from ginger-laden cliffs into clear, fern-banked

Molokai

Kaunakakai

Maui

Lahaina

Kahului

Haleakala
10,023'

Hana

Lanai

Kahoolawe

Hawaii

Waimea

Mauna Kea
13,796'

Hilo

Kailua

Mauna Loa
13,680'

pools. Billowing fields of sugar cane and neat rows of pineapple spread over thousands of fertile acres.

The major islands today are the eight that lie at the southeastern end of the chain. Seven of these are inhabited; the eighth, Kahoolawe, is used by the Navy for bombing and gunnery practice. Hawaii is the largest island–and is usually referred to as "the Big Island." With an area of 4,035 square miles, it is almost twice as large as all of the other Hawaiian islands combined. The Big Island boasts two mountain peaks that rise more than 13,000 feet from sea level, two active volcanoes, and a national park. Its varied climate and terrain provide great contrasts in scenery: sugar plantations, truck farms, cattle ranches, resorts, lush fern forests, orchards, flower fields, coffee plantations, and great expanses of lava.

Maui is the second largest island. It has some of the most magnificent beaches in Hawaii, a variety of resort areas, a refurbished whaling port, and the vast, colorful crater of dormant Haleakala.

West and northwest of Maui, the islands of Lanai and Molokai are quiet and comparatively undeveloped. Most of Lanai is owned by Dole Pineapple Company. Visitors are welcome, but tourist facilities are almost nonexistent. Much of Molokai is ranch land, though resort development is beginning.

Oahu, third island in size, is first in number of people. Honolulu, the state capital, is located here, as are such famous landmarks as Diamond Head, Waikiki, and Pearl Harbor.

Westernmost of the main islands are Kauai and Niihau. Kauai is a mixture of sugar cane fields, resort areas, homes, and ranches. Lush vegetation blankets its mountains. Its volcanic summit, Waialeale, receives more than 400 inches of rainfall annually and is reputed to be the wettest place on earth. Tiny Niihau is privately owned and can be visited only by special invitation. Its residents are mostly pure Hawaiians who live simply, without electricity, automobiles, or television.

Stretching beyond Niihau is a series of tiny islets and atolls officially named the Northwestern Hawaiian Islands but still commonly called the Leeward Islands. Volcanic activity began at this end of the chain. Kure and Midway are the oldest of the islands; Hawaii, where volcanic activity still continues, is the youngest. The islands at the northwest are estimated to be five to ten million years old, the main islands two to five million. Military installations on French Frigate Shoals, Midway, and Kure are the only marks of human habitation in the northwestern group.

The islands from Nihoa to Pearl and Hermes Reef comprise the Hawaiian Islands National Wildlife Refuge, established in 1909 to protect some of the most important sea bird nesting colonies in the world. Four endangered species of birds—the Laysan duck, Laysan finch, Nihoa finch, and Nihoa millerbird—are protected here, and the bare slopes and steep cliffs of these remote land bits are home to thousands of other birds. Also protected here are the rare Hawaiian monk seal and the green sea turtle.

The most generally accepted theory on the origins of the people who first settled in the Hawaiian Islands is that they came from Southeast Asia, following routes that took them down through the islands of Indonesia. From there they continued their migrations eastward to island dots in the vast Pacific. Eventually these early explorers reached all of the island groups in the Polynesian triangle formed by New Zealand at the southwest, Easter Island at the southeast, and the Hawaiian Islands at the north. It is thought that the first Polynesians to reach Hawaii sailed up from the Marquesas about 750 A.D. Heavy migrations from Tahiti came later, during the 12th and 13th centuries.

The voyagers traveled in huge double-hulled canoes, 60 to 80 feet long. A center platform between the hulls supported a thatched hut for shelter. They brought with them pigs, chickens, dogs, and plants that would provide food both during the long sea journey and in their new land. These early Hawaiians introduced many plants to the islands, including taro, which was their principal food crop, bananas, breadfruit, coconuts, sugar cane, yams, sweet potatoes, and mountain apples.

Somehow the islands of the Hawaiian archipelago eluded the European navigators of the 16th and 17th centuries. It was not until January 18, 1778, that English explorer Captain James Cook, on his third voyage in the Pacific, came upon the western end of the Hawaiian chain, sighting first Kauai, then Oahu, then Niihau. Cook made his first landing at Waimea on the island of Kauai. After a fortnight in the islands—which he named the Sandwich Islands in honor of his patron, the fourth Earl of Sandwich—he sailed on to Alaska.

In November, Captain Cook returned to the tropical shores he had discovered earlier. This time he sighted Maui, Molokai, and lastly, the big island of Hawaii at the eastern end of the chain. On January 17, 1779, his two ships,

the *Discovery* and the *Resolution,* sailed into Kealakekua Bay. Here the natives welcomed him as their god Lono, whose special celebration was held during the *makahiki,* or harvest, season—the time when Captain Cook chanced to appear.

Cook left the islands again on February 4 but soon returned after a sudden storm hit the ships off the coast of Kohala, collapsing the foremast of the *Resolution.* Ten days later, on February 14, the captain died at the edge of the bay—clubbed and stabbed to death during an altercation between his men and the natives, involving a cutter stolen from one of the ships.

At the time of Captain Cook's arrival, the islands were divided into four kingdoms, each with a ruling chief. Wars were frequent among them. Kalaniopuu was chief of the island of Hawaii. His nephew, a young warrior from Kohala by the name of Kamehameha, was destined to become ruler of the entire island chain and the first of the eight monarchs that were to rule the island kingdom.

When the aging Kalaniopuu neared death, he named his highest-born son, Kiwalao, as his successor. To Kamehameha he gave the guardianship of the family war god, Kukailimoku. It was not long before strife developed between Kiwalao and Kamehameha. In a battle in 1782, Kiwalao was killed, but it took Kamehameha nine more years to gain control of all of the island of Hawaii. One by one, the other islands fell to Kamehameha. Early in 1795, he captured Maui, Lanai, and Molokai. In mid-April he landed his canoes at Waikiki on Oahu.

Victory over the Oahuans came after a bloody battle in which Kamehameha's forces drove the enemy inland and trapped them at the edge of the steep cliffs

of Nuuanu Pali, where many were killed and many more leaped to their deaths. Now, all of the islands were under Kamehameha's rule except for Kauai and Niihau, and these came into his realm peacefully in April 1810 when Kaumualii, king of Kauai, entered into a pact with Kamehameha making Kauai a tributary kingdom in which Kaumualii would continue to govern Kauai but would accept Kamehameha's sovereignty.

For 77 years, Kamehamehas ruled the island kingdom. Their reign ended on December 11,1872, when Kamehameha V, a bachelor, died on the morning of his 43rd birthday. He left no heir to the throne and had named no successor. The next sovereign, William Lunalilo, was chosen by the Legislature. When he too died a bachelor, the Legislature elected David Kalakaua to rule the islands. Upon Kalakaua's death, his sister, Liliuokalani, took the throne. She reigned until the monarchy was overthrown on January 17, 1893. A provisional government then ruled the islands until the Republic of Hawaii was established on July 4, 1894.

As more and more foreigners landed in the islands, foreign intervention in Hawaiian affairs became extensive, and so did rivalry for favors. Ships of England, France, Russia, and the United States made frequent visits to island ports, and Hawaii became a popular wintering place for ships en route to China with cargoes of furs collected during the summer along the northwest coast of the U.S. mainland. Trade in sandalwood thrived from 1811 until the supply was exhausted in 1830. Then whaling took over as the mainstay of Hawaii's economy, and whaleships flocked to Hawaiian ports.

During the first half of the 19th century, a number of foreign powers made attempts to establish their positions in the islands. In 1816 the Russians erected a fort at Waimea on Kauai. The following year they were expelled by the king of Kauai under strict orders from Kamehameha. Protestant missionaries arrived in Hawaii from Boston in April of 1820 and began to teach the natives Christian principles, reading, writing, and arithmetic, and the rudiments of democracy. France's interest in the islands was expressed by the arrival of the first Roman Catholic missionaries from France in 1827. For five months in 1843, the islands were actually under the British flag after they were seized by a British naval officer, Lord George Paulet. The British government later disavowed Paulet's act, and the kingdom was returned to Kamehameha III.

Beginning in 1840, negotiations got under way to assure Hawaii's independence. On November 28, 1843, Britain and France signed a declaration recognizing the independence of the Hawaiian kingdom. The following summer, the United States reaffirmed its recognition of Hawaii's independence.

The whaling industry, which reached its peak in 1852, went into a steady decline following the discovery of petroleum in Pennsylvania in 1859.

Introduction  11

Misfortunes helped to bring about its demise, including a growing scarcity of whales and the losses of many whaling ships during the Civil War. The death blow to the industry came in 1871 when 33 ships, including seven of Hawaiian registry, were lost when they became trapped in Arctic ice north of Bering Strait.

Conversion to agriculture came about gradually. Sugar led the way–the top-ranking crop then as it is today. The first successful plantation was opened in 1835 at Koloa, Kauai. Other mills followed, and other crops were planted. The sugar industry expanded rapidly following the signing of a reciprocity treaty between Hawaii and the United States in 1875, permitting duty-free exchange of products between the two countries. Rice was grown to supply the needs of the Chinese. Coffee plantations were started on Kauai, Oahu, and on the Big Island. There were short-lived attempts to grow tobacco, cotton, wheat, and potatoes, and to raise silkworms for a silk industry. Cattle ranches covered many acres of the Big Island and Maui. Some pineapple was grown, though the pineapple industry did not really get under way until the early 1900s after the Hawaiian Pineapple Company was organized by James D. Dole in 1901.

The mid-19th century brought extensive growth in agriculture and trade in Hawaii. It also brought a shortage of laborers needed to work on the plantations. There simply were not enough Hawaiians to fill the need. In 1852

the first Chinese laborers were brought to the islands under five-year contracts. Other races followed—the first Japanese in 1868, Portuguese from Madeira and the Azores in 1878, Spanish in 1898, Koreans and Filipinos in the early 1900s. Some of these immigrants returned to their homelands after their contracts expired, but many stayed on in the islands. Some went into business for themselves. Many married Hawaiian women, and over the generations racial strains have become more and more complex. Today pure Hawaiians and part Hawaiians make up only one sixth of the state's population. One fourth of Hawaii's people are of mixed blood strains.

During the reign of Queen Liliuokalani, strong feelings grew among island businessmen favoring the annexation of Hawaii to the United States. The Spanish-American War finally convinced the United States government of the strategic position of the Hawaiian Islands in the Pacific and helped to turn the tide in favor of annexation. The sovereignty of the Republic was transferred in a ceremony at Iolani Palace at noon on August 12, 1898. However, it was not until almost two years later, on June 14, 1900, that the territorial government actually went into effect and Sanford B. Dole was appointed governor.

The struggle for statehood for Hawaii began as early as 1903. The first statehood bill was introduced in 1919, and others followed with regularity after that. Efforts at statehood were put aside during the tense period of World War II following Japan's surprise attack on Pearl Harbor on the morning of December 7, 1941. During the war years, Hawaii became America's defense post in the Pacific. Pearl Harbor was headquarters for the Pacific fleet, and Schofield Barracks was the largest Army post under the United States flag.

Efforts to gain statehood began again right after the war. But it was not until March 11, 1959, that Congress finally passed the enabling act. On August 21 of that year, President Dwight D. Eisenhower signed the proclamation that made the "Aloha State" the 50th star in the United States flag.

# aloha!

# Oahu

Oahu is an island of tremendous variety, of famous views and unexpected ones, historic landmarks and modern architectural achievements, mushrooming towns and wilderness areas, windy heights and tropical valleys, and a fascinating mélange of people and cultures. Colorful and friendly Honolulu, a sprawling city of more than 300,000 people, is a blend of South Seas, Orient, and modern American city, with a warmth and informality rarely seen on the mainland. Seat of Hawaiian government since 1850, it offers an intriguing look at Island history during monarchy, republic, territory, and statehood days. Honolulu Harbor, once a port of call for whalers and for fur and sandalwood traders, now shelters luxury liners and freighters from around the world. At Waikiki, sun-bronzed bodies dot the sands of a modern resort center that was the seaside playground of early Hawaiian monarchs. Behind Honolulu, rain-washed valleys cut the purple-tinged Koolau Range that forms a mountain spine roughly paralleling the eastern shore of the island. On the windward side of the mountains, suburban towns, farmland, lush pastures, and banana patches lie at the base of steep, green-clad ridges. To the west the older Waianae Mountains slope up from a plateau planted to pineapple and sugar cane. On the ocean side of these mountains, broad, arid valleys open to sandy shores.

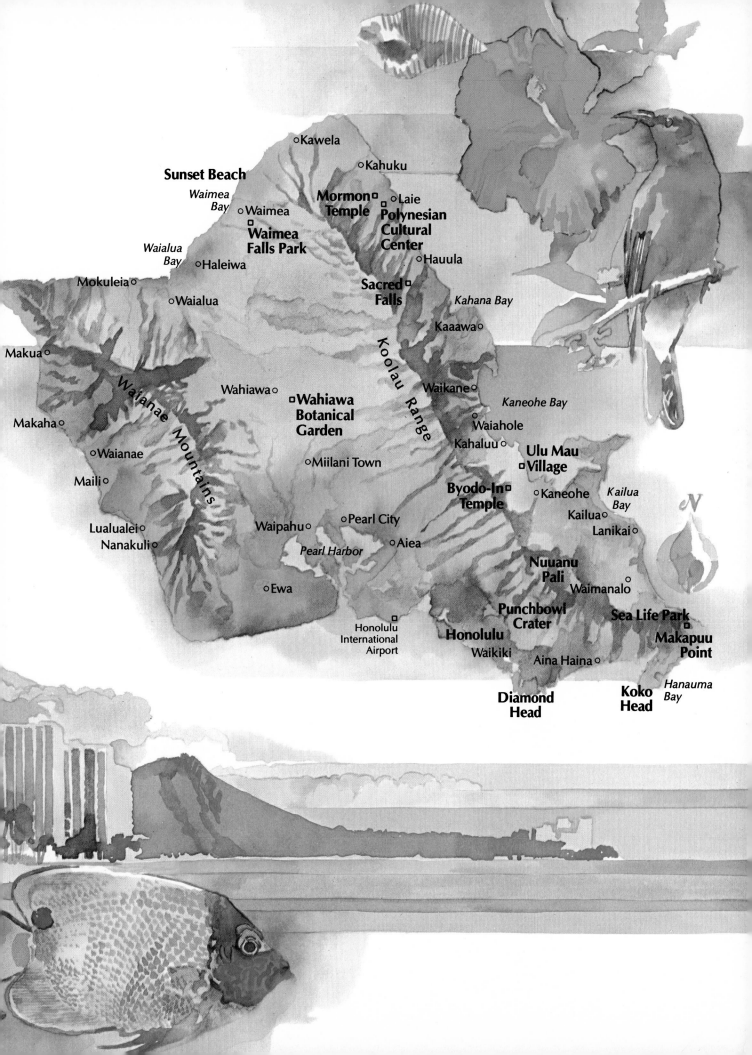

Kawela

Kahuku

Sunset Beach

*Waimea Bay* ○ Waimea

Mormon Temple □ ○ Laie

□ Polynesian Cultural Center

□ Waimea Falls Park

*Waialua Bay* ○ Haleiwa

○ Hauula

Mokuleia ○

○ Waialua

Sacred Falls □

*Kahana Bay*

Makua ○

Waianae Mountains

Kaaawa ○

Koolau Range

Wahiawa ○

□ Wahiawa Botanical Garden

Waikane ○

*Kaneohe Bay*

Makaha ○

○ Waiahole

Kahaluu ○

□ Ulu Mau Village

○ Waianae

○ Miilani Town

Maili ○

Byodo-In Temple □

○ Kaneohe

*Kailua Bay*

Kailua

Lanikai ○

Lualualei ○

○ Pearl City

Waipahu ○

Nanakuli ○

Aiea ○

*Pearl Harbor*

Nuuanu Pali

Waimanalo ○

Ewa ○

Punchbowl Crater

Sea Life Park □

Honolulu

Makapuu Point

Honolulu International Airport □

Waikiki

Aina Haina ○

Koko Head

*Hanauma Bay*

Diamond Head

N

# Honolulu...delightful mix of old and new

*A LOW-PROFILE HONOLULU spread a short distance back from the waterfront, and interisland steamers were a mode of transport between islands when these photographs were taken around the turn of the century. Today, sailors head their craft past high-rise buildings that dwarf the masts of pleasure boats tucked into Ala Wai Yacht Basin.*

# . . . Honolulu

*HONOLULU SPREADS over some 25 miles of Oahu's leeward shore and inland onto the ridges and into the valleys of the Koolau Range. Waikiki, tourist playground, covers a peninsula that extends from Ala Wai Yacht Harbor (left in photo) to Diamond Head (just out of picture at right), bordered on one side by the ocean and on the inland side by the Ala Wai Canal.*

TOM TRACY

# . . . Honolulu

ARIZONA MEMORIAL in Pearl Harbor, built over the hulk of the
sunken battleship, honors the 1,102 men entombed below.

TOM TRACY

*A SNUG HARBOR for ships since whaling days, Hawaii's major port is aptly named Honolulu, or "fair haven." Visitors arriving by sea today see these views of the downtown skyline. From piers adjacent to the Aloha Tower, the broad Ala Moana carries traffic past the business district toward Waikiki.*

Oahu **21**

*A WELCOME OASIS in the midst of urban development, watercress fields near Pearl Harbor supply about a third of the state's crop. Pickers in rubber boots and waterproof aprons work the patches, walking on tiles that divide the swampy fields. Island watercress is taller and milder than that grown on the mainland. Eleven acres of it are tended here.*

# . . . Honolulu

ELLIOTT VARNER SMITH

*TARO AND RICE, cultivated at Waipahu when the picture below was taken in 1910, fed workers in the Oahu Sugar Company's plantation town.*

BISHOP MUSEUM

Oahu **23**

ELLIOTT VARNER SMITH

*OLD AND NEW are frequent neighbors in downtown Honolulu. Sleek new towers to house Honolulu's business giants seem to spring up overnight, but the efforts of concerned citizens are resulting in the saving of many architectural treasures. Graceful coconut palms set off the 1929 Alexander & Baldwin building (above), which blends Hawaiian and Oriental features. At right, the T. R. Foster building, built in 1891, is enjoying new life as a restaurant.*

CRAIG AURNESS

**24** Oahu

# . . . Honolulu

OLD DOWNTOWN, along and just off Merchant Street, contains the oldest commercial buildings left in the city. One landmark is the 1870 Kamehameha V Post Office in the foreground below. The Yokohama Specie Bank building behind it was called the most handsome bank building in Honolulu when it was built in 1909.

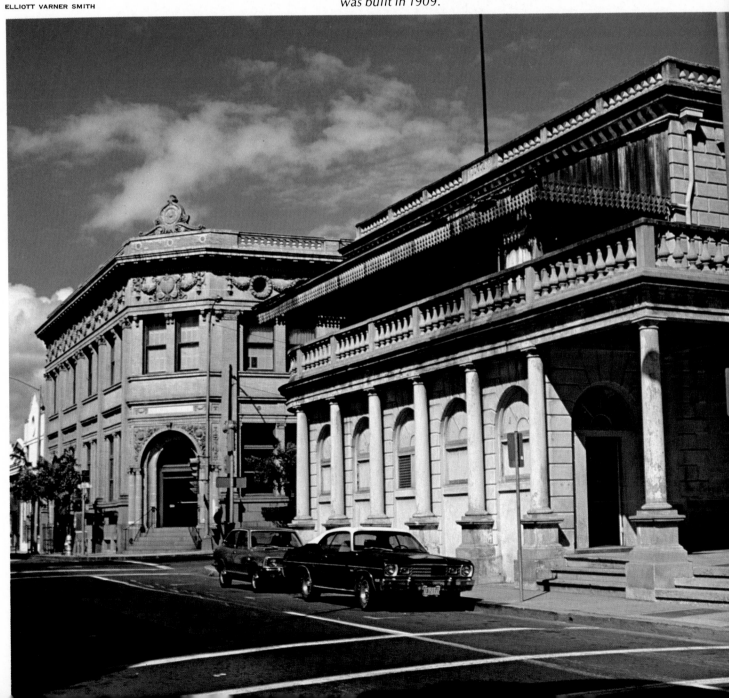

RICK WHITE

*MULE-DRAWN TRAM CAR of Hawaiian Tramways, Ltd., stops in front of the judiciary building, Aliiolani Hale, on a run from Houghtaling Road to Thomas Square. Electric trolleys replaced mule-cars in 1903.*

# . . . Honolulu

NOTEWORTHY DISPLAYS of color and plant material reward the visitor to these sites. Along the Pali Highway, the poinsettia hedge at left is a riot of crimson bloom from December to March. Rare exotic plants, magnificent trees, and outstanding orchids, bromeliads, and palms are among the special collections in Foster Garden (right). Below, Liliuokalani Garden is a delightful five-acre oasis not far from bustling downtown Honolulu.

CRAIG AURNESS

ED COOPER

Oahu **33**

# . . . Honolulu

*OPEN TO THE SKY and Island breezes, Hawaii's state
capitol, seen here from the lanai of Iolani Palace,
has a wonderful feeling of spaciousness and light.
Thirty-six cantilevered concrete ribs, with glass mosaic
between them, form the open crown of the building. From
the fifth floor, visitors can look down into the central
court and out to a view of city, sea, and mountains.*

Oahu **35**

*ONLY ROYAL PALACE in the United States, Iolani Palace was completed in 1879 during the reign of King David Kalakaua. On November 25, 1890, Kalakaua sailed for California, where he died two months later in San Francisco's Palace Hotel. His sister and successor to the throne, Queen Liliuokalani, occupied the Palace until the monarchy was overthrown in 1893. The building became the capitol for the Provisional Government, then for the Republic, the Territory, and the State of Hawaii.*

# Reminders of a unique heritage

*ENJOYING the Palace grounds about 1884, King Kalakaua and Queen Kapiolani pause near the coronation pavilion. Below, in an impressive annexation ceremony at the Palace shortly before noon on August 12, 1898, the sovereignty of the Republic was transferred to the United States.*

Oahu **37**

# . . . a unique heritage

*KAMEHAMEHA DAY PARADE on June 11 is part of a celebration honoring the ruler who unified the Islands. For the occasion, Island blossoms decorate the colorful floats, and Kamehameha's statue in front of the Judiciary Building is draped with 40-foot leis.*

*CORONATION PAVILION was built in 1883 for ceremonies in which King Kalakaua crowned himself and Queen Kapiolani. It is now the setting for Friday noontime concerts by the Royal Hawaiian Band. The pavilion dome is the original, but the termite-damaged foundation and pillars have been rebuilt of concrete. Eight pillars represent the eight major islands; the shields are designs based on various flags.*

# . . . a unique heritage

TOM TRACY

*HONOLULU'S PAST is brought to life in restored architectural treasures in the Civic Center. Missionaries from New England established the first Honolulu mission here in 1820 and built the Islands' first frame house (above) the following year from materials shipped around the Horn. Nearby Kawaiahao Church (left) was dedicated in 1842. The coral block structure was preceded by four thatched churches.*

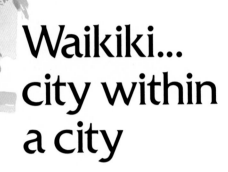

# Waikiki...
# city within
# a city

*COLORFUL WAIKIKI is where the action is. But lively as Waikiki is both day and night, it remains a place where it is possible to sit quietly and watch a sunset that is always different than it was the night before.*

Oahu **43**

TOM TRACY

CRAIG AURNESS

**44** Oahu

# . . . Waikiki

L. E. EDGEWORTH  BISHOP  MUSEUM

*WAIKIKI BEACH has not lost its popularity as a gathering place for
sun-seekers. In 1913, when the photograph above was taken, only private
residences and two hotels—the Moana (still peeking out today from
behind the palms in the photograph above left) and the Seaside (replaced
in 1926 by the palatial Royal Hawaiian Hotel, below left)—overlooked
the beach. Today, high-rise hotels border the shore all the way to Diamond
Head, and more visitors look for a place to stretch out on the sand; but
cares continue to disappear beneath the same warm sun beside the
same blue sea.*

# . . . Waikiki

*WHATEVER THE MOOD, Waikiki has something to suit it. When the sun is high, surfers, swimmers, and sunbathers enjoy the beach activities. At dusk, catamarans and other craft move quietly along the horizon. For visitors who prefer to absorb the scene from above, beachfront hotels provide dizzying views of the activity below.*

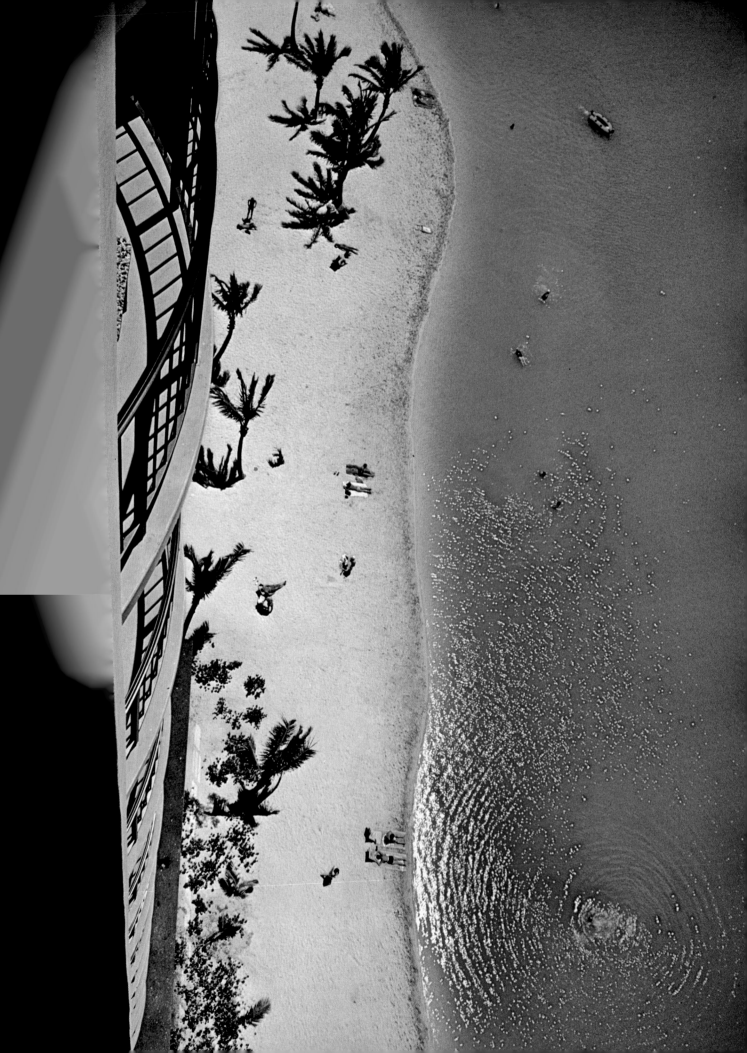

# Superb seascapes and a variety of marine life

ED ROBINSON

SEA LIFE PARK

AN ASTONISHING WORLD of marine life surrounds the Hawaiian Islands. Amateurs and experts alike study the sea's treasures. Because of its great clarity and extensive underwater life, Hanauma Bay (left) has been made a marine preserve. Butterfly fish (top), are only a sampling of what snorkelers may find in the crystal clear waters. At Sea Life Park (above), a pilot whale helps to hold a plumeria lei for the porpoises' powerful leaps.

Oahu **49**

# . . . marine life

*FISHING is a favorite pastime on all the Islands, and on almost every rocky point or sandy beach you will usually see someone dunking a line or tossing a net. The offshore waters are lucrative hunting grounds for spear fishermen.*

## 50  Oahu

# Behind the city...
# cool heights and
# misty valleys

*HIGHEST AND COOLEST of Honolulu's residential areas
spreads up the slope of Tantalus, volcanic peak that rises
above the central city. Here, beautiful homes are almost
hidden in lush vegetation, and panoramic views appear at many
a turn in the road. The city takes on a soft sunset glow in
the view from Puu Ualakaa State Park (left). Hill of Sacrifice,
or Puowaina, is the Hawaiian name for Punchbowl Crater (above),
where row on row of simple tablets mark the graves of some
22,000 war dead in the National Memorial Cemetery of the Pacific.*

Oahu **53**

# . . . behind the city

CRAIG AURNESS

A PLEASANT MEETING PLACE on the grounds
of the East-West Center, the structure above
was dedicated by the king of Thailand when he
visited the Center in 1967. It was constructed
first at the Bangkok Grand Palace, then dismantled
and reconstructed on its present site.

CRAIG AURNESS

**54** Oahu

CRAIG AURNESS

*EAST-WEST CENTER shares the University of Hawaii's Manoa Valley
campus. It was established in 1960 to promote cultural and technical
interchange among the peoples of Asia, the Pacific, and the United States.
The water basin at left is in the Center's tranquil Japanese garden
bordering Manoa Stream.*

# Through and over the mountains

*FROM THE PALI LOOKOUT (above), the breathtaking view is northward
along the fluted windward palisades to Mokolii, a small island at the tip
of Kaneohe Bay, and out to Mokapu Peninsula at the bay's southeastern end.
An easy drive today, the trip over the twisting Nuuanu Pali Road (left above)
in 1913 was a challenge to any touring buff. On the windward side of the
mountains, in the early 1880s, a narrow-gauge railroad (left) moved cane
to Waimanalo Beach for shipment by steamers to Honolulu.*

Oahu **57**

# . . . over the mountains

IN A BEAUTIFUL SETTING, with a backdrop of nearly vertical cliffs, the Pali Golf Course is just about 30 minutes from Waikiki. Hawaii's golfers can tee off by the sea or on volcanic slopes on a variety of courses that offer almost ideal conditions for year-round play.

TOM TRACY

**58** Oahu

TOM TRACY

*TWIN TUNNELS of the Pali Highway pierce the Koolaus. Above the freeway, part of the old cross-island road winds along the windward cliff below Pali Lookout. Originally an old Hawaiian footpath, it was improved for horses in 1845, later widened for carriages, and still later improved a little more for cars.*

Oahu **59**

# Around the Koolaus

DAVID CORNWELL

*THE VALLEY OF THE TEMPLES features the above replica of the 900-year-old Byodo-In Temple in Japan. Hundreds of brilliantly hued carp (opposite), called koi by the Japanese, enliven its reflecting pond. Bred in Japan over many centuries from plain gray carp, these colorful fish, seen in landscape pools throughout Hawaii, are beloved pets and valuable possessions, symbolizing manliness and courage and said to bring good luck.*

Oahu **65**

ED COOPER

WINDSWEPT LAIE POINT juts into the sea
north of Hauula. From this rocky promontory,
you can watch the sea surging against the
undercut rocks and look for long distances
up and down the coast.

# . . . around the Koolaus

*A WINDWARD OAHU LANDMARK, the Mormon Temple below is part of a church development that takes in about 6,000 acres in the Laie area. It includes the town of Laie, the Polynesian Cultural Center, a branch campus of Brigham Young University, and the Temple, which is set off in a formal garden.*

# . . . around the Koolaus

*FRUIT STANDS on windward Oahu tempt travelers and shoppers with tropical delights such as bananas, papayas, mountain apples, and mangoes. Above, North Shore beach sands are ideal for youngsters' castle-building.*

*A MILE-LONG WALK through Waimea Arboretum offers a cool, refreshing respite during a round-the-island drive. For those who prefer to ride, open-air trams follow the same route.*

Oahu 69

*THE EASY PACE of old Hawaii is still felt on the North Shore. Small boats find a protected moorage here beneath the trees that overhang the banks of picturesque Anahulu Stream at Haleiwa, where missionaries settled in 1832.*

**70** Oahu

# A luxuriant landscape
# surrounds a wet heartland

# . . . a luxuriant landscape

DAVID MUENCH

*PLANT LIFE on Kauai varies from that found in cool, misty high altitudes to lush tropical jungle and some outstanding cultivated collections. Ferns and ohia thrive here on Waialeale's slopes.*

*WAIALEALE'S SUMMIT is usually obscured by low-hanging clouds that drop torrential rains of 400 to 600 inches a year atop the ancient volcano.*

BOONE MORRISON

# A parkland of unforgettable beauty

DAVID MUENCH

# A South Seas setting on the north shore

*REWARDS FOR BEACHCOMBERS are few on a tranquil day like this one, but when the sea becomes turbulent, these north shore beaches often yield wave-tossed treasures.*

**88** Kauai

*PANDANUS-LADEN CLIFFS overhang the shore near Hanalei. Rock-edged coves stretch west from here, but strong offshore currents make swimming dangerous except in a few places.*

# . . . the north shore

ELLIOTT VARNER SMITH

*TARO PLANTS mature 18 to 24
months after they are planted
in the irrigated plots. Poi is made
by cooking and pounding the heavy
corms. The huge leaves may be
cooked and served like spinach and
are also used to wrap foods for
steaming (lau laus).*

ELLIOTT VARNER SMITH

*HEART-SHAPED LEAVES of taro plants blanket
the valley through which the Hanalei River threads
its way down from forested mountains. Taro was
the most important food crop of the early Polynesian
settlers who brought many varieties of the plant
to their new homeland. Today Kauai grows the most
taro of all the islands.*

DAVID MUENCH

Kauai **91**

# Na Pali...bold precipices hide magnificent valleys

ROBERT WENKAM

TARO GROWS WILD beneath gnarled
kukui trees and alongside tumbling
streams that once provided water
for taro patches cultivated on
stone-walled terraces by Hawaiians
who lived in these valleys.

ROBERT WENKAM

MASSIVE CLIFFS rise 2,000
to 3,000 feet from the sea on
the rugged Na Pali Coast.

BILL GLEASNER

# . . . Na Pali

ROBERT WENKAM

*BEACHES that disappear
when the sea sometimes pounds
these shores nestle beneath
towering black lava cliffs.
Refreshing streams tumble down
Waialeale's slopes, following
boulder-strewn courses to the
sea and providing cooling
dips for hikers following the
strenuous Kalalau Trail.*

*DWARFED BY THE SCENERY, a tiny
helicopter skims the Na Pali Coast,
providing views of remote valleys
where magnificent waterfalls drop
over sheer cliffs to the luxuriant jungle
below. Sightseeing tours over the valleys have become a well-publicized
Kauai specialty.*

BILL GLEASNER

BILL GLEASNER

Kauai **95**

*BODY SURFERS tumble shoreward on a good wave at Brennecke's Beach on the south shore. This is Kauai's most popular body surfing beach. Nearby are good board surfing areas and calm waters for swimmers.*

# The sunny south shore

GENTLE WAVES provide thrills enough for these happy youngsters at Poipu Beach. Several resort hotels and condominium complexes are clustered here on Kauai's south shore around reef-protected coves favored by swimmers and snorkelers.

# . . . the south shore

COARSE SALT, scooped from shallow ponds after the sea water evaporates, seasons many dishes served in the Islands. Early Hawaiians used the salt to preserve their meat and fish. These ponds are near Salt Pond Park, which was named for them.

ELLIOTT VARNER SMITH

INVITING BACK COUNTRY, legends, and history abound on the windward side of Kauai. The main highway bypasses the serene countryside above, but side roads from Kapaa and Kealia meander through it. Just north of the Wailua River, the coconut grove at far left was planted in 1896 near a lagoon that was a fishpond for Hawaiian royalty. The Hole in the Mountain (left) is said to have been made when a great chief threw his spear with such force that it went right through this mountain ridge near Anahola.

Kauai **103**

# ...the east side

*FIRM SANDS of Kalapaki Beach appeal to joggers and sunbathers while swimmers nearby enjoy the clear, protected waters of the bay.*

*EASILY ACCESSIBLE and probably the most beautiful waterfall on Kauai, Opaekaa Falls spills in a lacy pattern of silver over a cliff cloaked in greenery.*

Kauai **105**

# Garden viewing on the "Garden Island"

*UNUSUAL GARDENS await the visitor to
Kauai. Eight garden areas comprise Olu Pua
Gardens (above), formerly the estate of
a plantation manager. Cacti, succulents,
and an extensive collection of African
aloes are included in Plantation Gardens
(right). A center of research in tropical
botany and horticulture, the Pacific Tropical
Botanical Garden covers 186 hillside
acres above the Lawai Valley (opposite).*

# . . . the Valley Island

ED COOPER

*GREEN-CLAD WALLS of Iao Valley cut into the center of Puu Kukui, second rainiest peak in Hawaii. Three miles from Wailuku, the road ends at Iao Needle (above), a 2,250-foot pinnacle that juts up from the floor of a hushed, often cloud-draped ravine. At Kepaniwai Heritage Gardens (left), a county park in the valley, gardens and pavilions represent the cultures that were instrumental in the growth of the Islands.*

Maui **113**

WHATEVER THE INTERESTS, Maui's
beaches seem able to please. Surfers,
both beginning and expert, find waves;
tidepools offer intriguing discoveries;
sands are soft beneath the feet.
For less active beach-goers, clouds that
gather over the West Maui Mountains
(above) make sky-watching as fascinating
as wave-watching.

**114** Maui

# The lure of sand and surf

PHOTOGRAPHS BY ELLIOTT VARNER SMITH

# Cane fields slope to the mountains

*FIELDS OF RIPPLING SUGAR CANE cloak the foothills and plains of central and western Maui. Brought to Hawaii in the canoes of the first arrivals, sugar cane was growing wild when Captain Cook arrived in 1778. Now it is a major crop on the four largest islands. All but about 3 percent of the sugar produced in Hawaii is shipped raw for processing on the mainland.*

TOM TRACY

116  Maui

# West Maui...
# history, shopping,
# resorts

*NOT LACKING in diversions, Lahaina offers an 1890-style train to ride; ample subjects for artists and photographers; and snack shops in which to sample such local specialties as macadamia nut ice cream.*

Maui **123**

# . . . West Maui

GOLF COURSES AND BEACHES are attractions
on the flanks of the West Maui Mountains and
the western slope of Haleakala. Here at Kaanapali,
at Kapalua to the north, and at Wailea to the
south, golfers face challenging courses overlooking
beaches that are among the best in Hawaii.

ELLIOTT VARNER SMITH

TOM TRACY

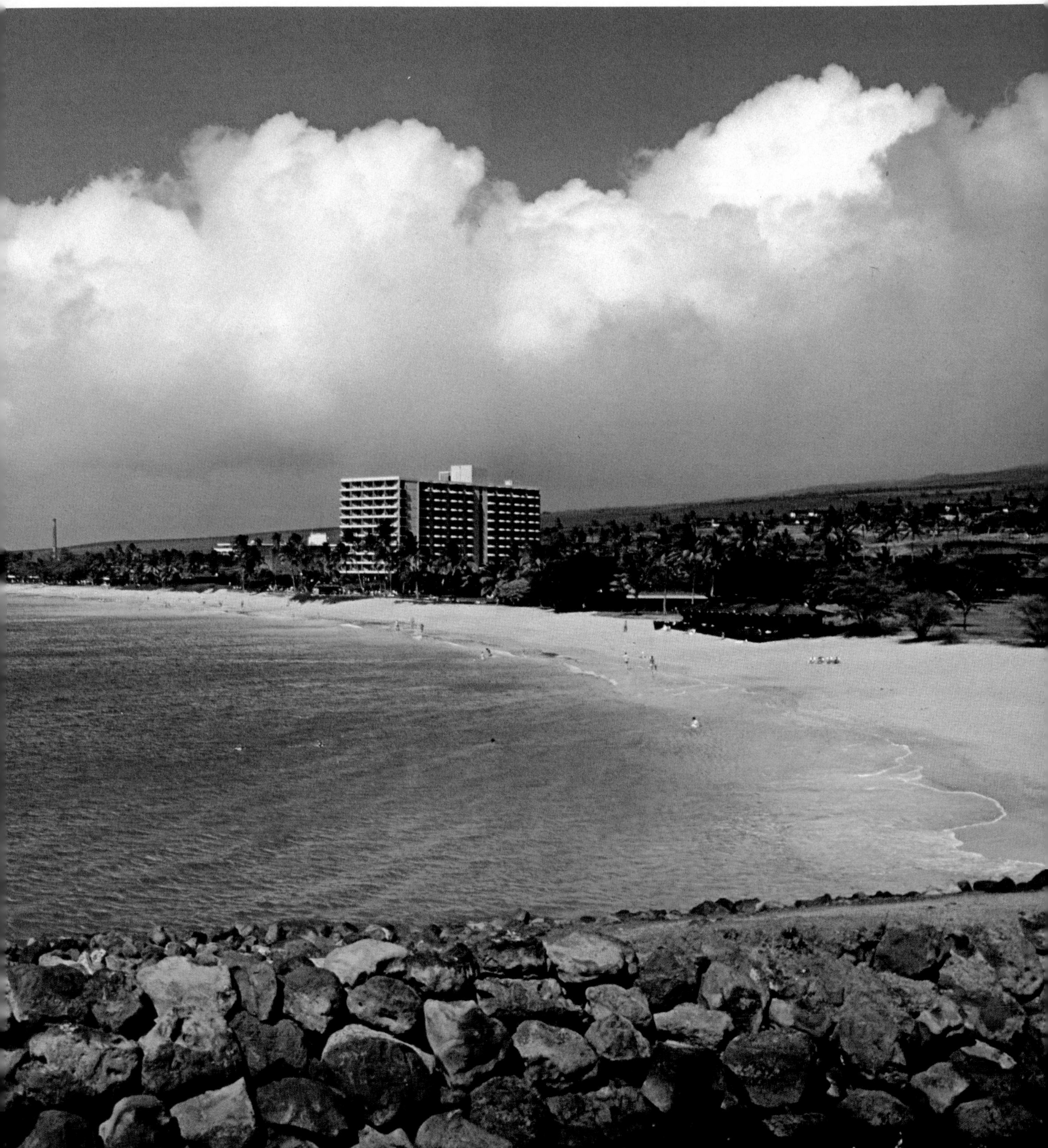

*THE SEA'S MOODS are always fascinating. Here a slight breeze ripples the water off Lahaina, and the sun's rays penetrate the heavy cloud cover, casting a soft glow over this tranquil late-day scene.*

**126** Maui

# Sailors and whales share the waters

JOSEPH SAITTA

*WHALE WATCHING is a popular pastime
each year during the winter months
when the frolicsome humpback whales
return to their courting, birthing, and
nursing grounds in the waters between
Maui, Molokai, Lanai, and Kahoolawe.*

JAMES HUDNALL, JR.

# Haleakala...fertile slopes and a vast crater

ON THE COOL SLOPES of Haleakala, flowers and vegetables thrive. Breeze-cooled pastures with magnificent views down to the sea are delightful places for horseback rides. Farmers grow cucumbers, tomatoes, cabbages, and the famous mild-flavored onions that are an Island favorite. Carnation fields on the mountainside yield cut flowers and lei blossoms for Honolulu markets.

Maui **129**

# . . . Haleakala

*PORTUGUESE IMMIGRANTS were among the settlers who farmed the productive fields of Maui's Kula district in the 1800s and were the original parishioners of the quaint, octagonal Catholic Church of the Holy Ghost (above), built in 1897 on the tranquil slopes of the mountain. The church altar was made in Austria and shipped in sections around Cape Horn. The weathered wood facades of stores along Makawao's main street (right) contribute to the "Old West" atmosphere of this photogenic upcountry town.*

*FROM THE LOWER SLOPE of Haleakala, golfers at Wailea look across the channel to Lanai.*

DOROTHY KRELL

TOM TRACY

# . . . Haleakala

ROBERT WENKAM

SUBTLY TINTED symmetrical cones
rise from a painted wasteland
within Haleakala, the "House of the
Sun." According to Hawaiian legend,
the demigod Maui once snared the sun
from the rim of this volcano and made it
promise to go more slowly across the
sky to give his mother's tapa cloth more
time to dry. The silversword plant
(right) is protected here. The rare
plant grows for 4 to 20 years before it
sends up its single 1 to 9-foot flower
stalk. After one short season of
bloom, from about May to September, the
plant sends out seeds, then dies.

ROBERT WENKAM

THE NENE, Hawaii's state bird,
had become almost extinct when a
breeding project was started some
25 years ago. Since then, several
hundred birds have been released
on Mauna Loa and here on Haleakala,
where about 150 nene now live
in the crater.

Maui 133

DAVID MUENCH

# East Maui's jungled coast

A JUNGLE of tropical plant material,
including thick groves of bamboo (above)
and several varieties of ginger (right),
thrives along the roadside and in several
wayside parks along the Hana Highway.

**134** Maui

CLIFF HOLLENBECK

*TWISTING AND DEMANDING, but a worthwhile adventure, the Hana Highway (above) coils along a sea-lashed coast, clinging to forested cliffs, burrowing into gulches draped with waterfalls, and crossing streams on narrow concrete bridges that date back more than half a century. Warty-skinned breadfruit trees (left) along the way are easily identifiable; the fruit is good baked or steamed.*

DARROW M. WATT

Maui **135**

# . . . East Maui

RONALD A. SITTON

UNFORGETTABLE VIEWS appear at every
turn of the road. A spur road leads down
to a quiet settlement on the Keanae
Peninsula (above), where people work the
swampy taro fields and fish from a
foam-splashed shore. Keanae's coral stone
church (left) is more than 100 years old.
Wailua Falls (far left) cascades down
Haleakala's wet windward slope and pours
over a jungled cliff to enter the sea at
Wailua Cove. Paved road continues
beyond Hana to the famous Seven Pools
section of Haleakala National Park.

RONALD A. SITTON

DAVID MUENCH

Maui **137**

# . . . East Maui

COWS GRAZE PEACEFULLY on Lyons Hill (above) near St. Mary's Catholic
Church. The steeple to the right of the Catholic Church is that of
Wananalua Congregational Church, established in 1837. Constructed by
hand of lava rock over a period of 20 years, Wananalua is one of the
oldest churches in the Islands. On the opposite page, at top, cane fields
blanketed the slopes near Wananalua Church and the Hana Sugar Mill in
1904. In 1940, ranching replaced sugar as the major industry. At bottom,
in the view from Lyons Hill, sailboats lie quietly at anchor in the calm
water of Hana Bay. Kauiki Head rises at the edge of the bay.

# Molokai

Tourism is just beginning to touch the Friendly Isle. New residential and resort areas are under development, but most of Molokai is still a rural landscape. The island was formed by two major volcanic domes. The tableland called Mauna Loa at the western end, which rises to only 1,381 feet, was the first to build up. The jagged mountains in the northeast, topped by 4,940-foot Kamakou, were formed later by the East Molokai volcano. A much younger volcano, Kauhako, created a flat tongue of land that juts out from the north coast, isolated from the rest of the island by fortresslike cliffs. Leprosy victims were exiled there for almost a century. Molokai has many attractions for outdoorsmen. Campers can choose from beautiful sites in mountain meadows, on the banks of sparkling streams, and along the ocean's edge. Hikers can explore green-carpeted valleys where Hawaiian taro farmers and fishermen once lived and where bananas, mangoes, sugar cane, taro, and ginger grow wild and waterfalls drop from towering cliffs. Hunters can go after animals and game birds, and the submarine shelf at Molokai's southwest corner is one of Hawaii's most fertile fishing grounds.

Moomon
Beac

Kepuhi Beach

Molokai
Ranch

Maunaloa

Mauna Loa
1,381'

**Palaau Park** □

○ Kalaupapa

**Kalawao Park** ○

**Lamaloa Head**

Halawa Valley

Waikolu Valley

Pelekunu Valley

Wailau Valley

Puu O Hoku Ranch

Kalae ○

Kualapuu ○

Olokui 4,602'

Kamakou 4,970'

○ Waialua

○ Kaunakakai

Pukoo ○

*N*

○ Kamalo

# The quiet life on Molokai

*TRADING CENTER for Molokai, little Kaunakakai is a lively, friendly place. The old wooden buildings along its wide main street offer everything from local food specialties to the latest gossip. Above, low tide brings people to the shallow waters off the south shore where bait fish are easily netted.*

PLANTED BY KAMEHAMEHA V more than 100 years ago, the coconut trees in this extensive grove near Kaunakakai now shade a shoreside park. One of the foods brought to the Islands by the first Polynesian settlers, coconuts thrived in their new land. The hard shell of the nut encloses the white meat of the coconut and a milky fluid (coconut milk). At left, a young tree sprouts from a fallen nut.

# . . . the quiet life

MANY HANDS are needed at a hukilau. Everyone
pitches in to spread the huge net in a wide
circle near shore. The net is then hauled
shoreward, encircling the trapped fish. Everyone
who helps with the work shares in the catch.

PHOTOGRAPHS BY ELLIOTT VARNER SMITH (BOTTOM FAR LEFT, TOP
LEFT), TOM TRACY (CENTER), JO ANN MASAOKA (ABOVE, LEFT)

Molokai **145**

# A devoted priest served a lonely settlement

BILL GLEASNER

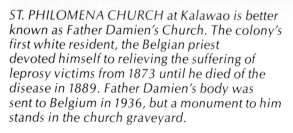

*ST. PHILOMENA CHURCH at Kalawao is better known as Father Damien's Church. The colony's first white resident, the Belgian priest devoted himself to relieving the suffering of leprosy victims from 1873 until he died of the disease in 1889. Father Damien's body was sent to Belgium in 1936, but a monument to him stands in the church graveyard.*

**146** Molokai

*A UNIQUE WAY to visit isolated Kalaupapa is to ride a mule down the steep, switchback trail that is the only land route to the settlement. Strangers are welcome now on the tiny peninsula that was a place of banishment for lepers from 1866 until sulfone drugs were discovered in 1946. The 4½-square-mile peninsula is isolated by pounding surf, a rocky coast, steep lava cliffs. The view down from the clifftop park that overlooks it shows the reason for Kalaupapa's name, which translates as "the leafy plain."*

Molokai **147**

ED COOPER

*ONLY A FEW ROADS crisscross Molokai. Destinations at the ends of two of them take visitors through quiet grazing land to beaches on the east and west coasts. From the ranch at the eastern end, a rough road zigzags down into Halawa Valley (above), where falls drop over green-clad cliffs to fill a stream that meanders out to the sea. At the west end of the island, a resort complex fronts 3 miles of sandy shore at Kepuhi Beach (right).*

**148** Molokai

# At the ends of the roads

TOM TRACY

TOM TRACY

Molokai **149**

# Rugged valleys notch the windward shore

ED COOPER

150 Molokai

ED COOPER

*THE PALI COAST from Kalaupapa to Halawa is one of the most spectacular
coastlines in Hawaii. Towering green cliffs ribboned with waterfalls plunge
hundreds of feet into the ocean. From boulder-strewn beaches, wet, untrodden
valleys slice deep into jagged mountains that reach their highest point
at 4,970-foot-high Kamakou.*

Molokai **151**

# Lanai

This small island, just a half-hour by air from Honolulu, is most known for pineapples, and pineapple does indeed cover acres and acres of Lanai's slopes. But for those who find pleasure in quiet surroundings and who like to explore little-traveled, undeveloped shores, Lanai has more than pineapples to offer. The island is the remains of an old volcanic peak that rises to more than 3,000 feet at Lanaihale, its high point. On the west side, a cultivated plateau ends in jagged cliffs that drop off to the sea. On the windward side, luxuriant gulches slope to a half-mile-wide coastal plain where reef-protected shoals offer good spear and net fishing, deserted shores reward beachcombers, and remains of old Hawaiian villages wait to be explored. Grassy knolls on Lanai's rolling hillsides are ideal picnic sites, with fine views over the slopes and across the water to other islands; and Lanai's weathered boulders bear some of Hawaii's best petroglyphs.

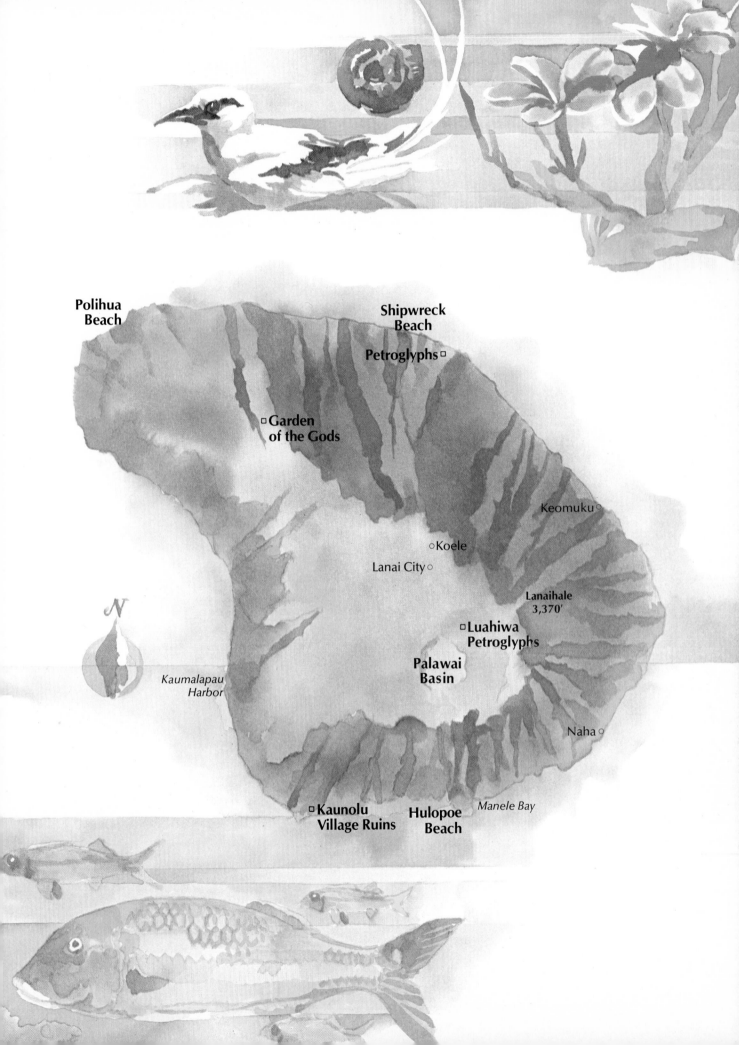

**Polihua Beach**

**Shipwreck Beach**

**Petroglyphs** □

□ **Garden of the Gods**

Keomuku ○

○ Koele

Lanai City ○

Lanaihale
3,370'

□ **Luahiwa Petroglyphs**

**Palawai Basin**

*N*

*Kaumalapau Harbor*

Naha ○

□ **Kaunolu Village Ruins**

**Hulopoe Beach**

*Manele Bay*

# Pineapples and quiet beauty

ROW AFTER ROW of pineapple plants spread over Lanai's landscape. More than 15,000 acres of this small island are planted in pineapples, Hawaii's second largest agricultural crop. The ripe fruit is harvested by hand and barged to Oahu, where, during the peak of the harvest, the largest pineapple cannery processes more than 3 million pineapples a day. Large quantities of fresh pineapples are airlifted directly to mainland markets, and many delighted tourists carry home their own fresh fruit.

CLIFF HOLLENBECK

**154** Lanai

# . . . contrasts

REMNANTS OF THE PAST and evidence of people long gone survive on Lanai's little-traveled shores. In an oasis of palm trees on the sandy windward coast, Keomuku village is a ghost town of a few old houses and the weathered church at left. Petroglyphs at Kukui Point (right) were discovered just a few years ago. Large round boulders like these were a favored surface for this early artwork. At Shipwreck Beach (below), a few hulks of old vessels lie rotting and rusting on the reef. The shore is littered with timbers and other remnants of once-proud vessels deliberately abandoned to this shallow reef graveyard.

NORMAN A. PLATE

CLIFF HOLLENBECK

ED COOPER

*QUIET WATERS of Manele Bay provide calm anchorage for pleasure craft and a tranquil setting for the fisherman dangling a line off the pier. The harbor is a popular destination for boats sailing across the channel from Lahaina on Maui's west coast.*

# A bay for swimmers and one for boats

*WAVES LAP gently at the edge of Hulopoe Beach, providing just enough excitement for these water babies.*

# Hawaii

Clouds brush the summits of Mauna Kea and Mauna Loa, the huge mountains that dominate the Big Island. Between mountain peaks and sea lie rain forests, weird lava formations, fertile grasslands, colorful gardens, orchards, truck farms, sugar and coffee plantations, and cattle ranches. The Neighbor Islands' largest town, Hilo, sprawls alongside crescent-shaped Hilo Bay. In the northwest corner of the island, a remarkably untouched bit of Hawaii survives in North Kohala, birthplace and boyhood home of the first Kamehameha. Up on the cool Waimea plateau, mists swirl over forest-capped hills and green grazing land. A few miles away, resort complexes lie along a dry, sunny coast. In beautiful, isolated valleys on the northeast coast, a luxuriant growth of native plants and trees is watered by abundant year-round rainfall and streams fed by winter snows that frequently dust Mauna Kea's summit. This big island, youngest in the Hawaiian chain, is still growing. Of the five volcanoes that formed Hawaii, two are still active. Mauna Loa, largest active volcano in the world, ended a 25-year quiet period with a summit eruption in 1975. Lively Kilauea, down on Mauna Loa's southeast flank, puts on frequent fiery shows, occasionally sending lava spilling all the way to the sea and adding more land area to an island already almost twice as large as all the other islands combined.

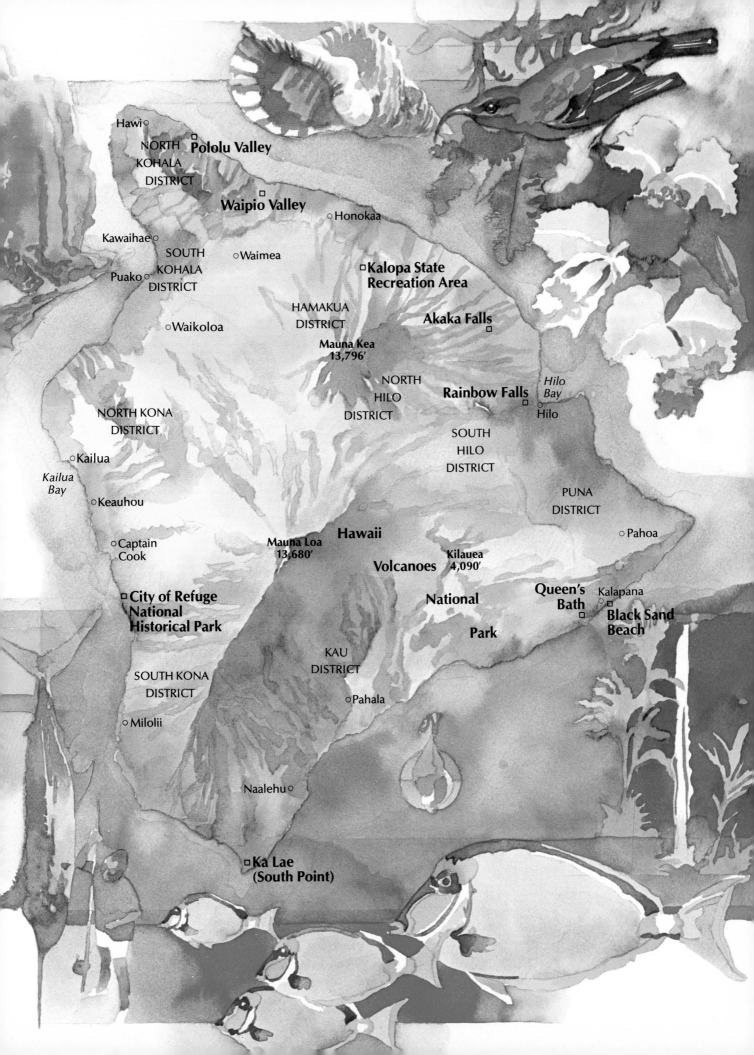

Hawi

NORTH
KOHALA
DISTRICT

**Pololu Valley**

**Waipio Valley**

Honokaa

Kawaihae

SOUTH
KOHALA
DISTRICT

Waimea

**Kalopa State
Recreation Area**

Puako

HAMAKUA
DISTRICT

**Akaka Falls**

Waikoloa

Mauna Kea
13,796'

NORTH
HILO
DISTRICT

**Rainbow Falls**

*Hilo
Bay*

Hilo

NORTH KONA
DISTRICT

SOUTH
HILO
DISTRICT

Kailua

*Kailua
Bay*

PUNA
DISTRICT

Keauhou

Pahoa

Captain
Cook

Mauna Loa
13,680'

**Hawaii**

Kilauea
4,090'

**Volcanoes**

**City of Refuge
National
Historical Park**

**National**

**Queen's
Bath**

Kalapana

**Park**

**Black Sand
Beach**

KAU
DISTRICT

SOUTH KONA
DISTRICT

Milolii

Pahala

Naalehu

**Ka Lae
(South Point)**

# Hilo...a city shaped by water

A DOUBLE CANOE drifts lazily on Hilo Bay, now a harbor for cruise ships and freighters from around the world.

ON A SPARKLING DAY, Mauna Kea is clearly visible beyond Hilo Bay. Pleasure boats lie at anchor where townspeople once set their nets at the waterfront of a sleepy little town (left). Now Hilo is the Islands' second largest town, spreading along the great arc of the bay and up Mauna Loa's slopes to about 1,500 feet.

FRANK DAVEY, BISHOP MUSEUM

Hawaii **167**

# . . . Hilo

*A MAGNIFICENT GREENBELT serves Hiloans along a waterfront where two tsunamis wreaked havoc. Hit hard by disastrous seismic waves in 1946 and 1960, Hilo has rebuilt its waterfront to include well-tended plantings, ponds and lagoons, and a bayside drive. Liliuokalani Gardens (left) cover almost 30 acres of the Waiakea Peninsula. Shaded picnic sites border Waiakea Pond (above).*

Hawaii **169**

*SAMPAN HARBOR (above) at the mouth of the Wailoa River shelters a good-sized fishing fleet. Spirited bidding takes place here when the catch is auctioned in the early morning. Later in the day, when work is done and the boats are washed clean, quiet descends and the harbor becomes a sleepy place. Not far away, there are fresh-water fish in the pond at Wailoa River State Park (right).*

**170** Hawaii

# The coast
# north of Hilo

*A COOL, GREEN GORGE is cut by Kolekole Stream in Akaka Falls State Park, a 66-acre arboretum of giant gingers, ferns, ti, azaleas, orchids, and bamboo. Ti plants frame a view of Akaka Falls (left), which drops in a silvery plume over a 442-foot precipice.*

Hawaii **173**

*STORM CLOUDS GATHER over Waipio Valley, an awesome gap in the rugged windward side of the Kohala Mountains. A four-wheel-drive road descends a steep mile from the lookout to the valley floor, resplendent with native plants and cut by a stream fed by waterfalls that drop from 2,000-foot-high cliffs. Opposite the lookout, an old horse trail zigzags up the bluff and crosses deeply furrowed tableland to the next big valley.*

**174** Hawaii

# . . . north of Hilo

*THE FULL FORCE of the sea strikes this windward coast. With no offshore reef to break the onslaught, ocean swells splash unchecked against jagged lava rocks.*

JOSEPH SAITTA

TOM TRACY

*JUNGLED GORGES cut the northeastern slope of Mauna Kea where the trade winds drop drenching rainfall. Canyons here are laced with waterfalls, and cliffs are overgrown with lush, tropical vegetation.*

**176** Hawaii

# . . . north of Hilo

*ON THE HAMAKUA COAST north of Hilo, taro farmers brought their crop out by mule train, and sugar cane arrived at the mill by wooden flume on a high trestle that spanned a deep gulch.*

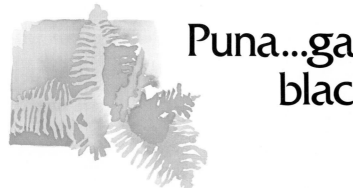

# Puna...gardens, orchards, black sand beaches

TOM TRACY

TOM TRACY

TOM TRACY

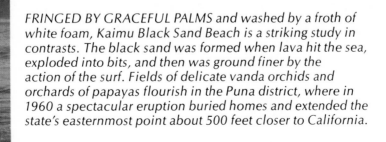

*FRINGED BY GRACEFUL PALMS and washed by a froth of white foam, Kaimu Black Sand Beach is a striking study in contrasts. The black sand was formed when lava hit the sea, exploded into bits, and then was ground finer by the action of the surf. Fields of delicate vanda orchids and orchards of papayas flourish in the Puna district, where in 1960 a spectacular eruption buried homes and extended the state's easternmost point about 500 feet closer to California.*

Hawaii **179**

# ... Puna

MACADAMIA NUT TREES grow almost to the sea in this commercial orchard south of Hilo. The trees produce an extremely hard-shelled nut that must be opened by a special cracking machine. The mouth-watering nuts are a Big Island specialty. Several factories conduct tours during which visitors can watch them being processed and packaged for shipment.

CLIFF HOLLENBECK

DAVID CORNWELL

Hawaii **181**

# . . . Puna

KEITH GUNNAR

SCULPTURED by the elements,
Puna's lava bluffs change
constantly. Many provide
good perches for fishermen,
who are often rewarded when
they dangle a line.

ED COOPER

**182** Hawaii

ANTHURIUMS thrive in the delicate shade cover
provided by tree ferns. The waxy blooms rank
number one in Big Island flower sales and are a
part of almost every home garden on the island.

DAVID MUENCH

# Volcanoes...famous Big Island attraction

JOSEPH SAITTA

*A POOL OF MOLTEN LAVA bubbles on the floor of Halemaumau (above). An awesome sight during a time of volcanic activity, fountains of fire, sometimes hundreds of feet high, illuminate Halemaumau's lava walls. Lava oozed down the mountain in 1971, blanketing a portion of the Chain of Craters Road (left) and cutting off access to the main part of the park from the coast section. The road has since been rebuilt. It reopened in the summer of 1979, making possible once again a 90-mile loop drive from Hilo through both the coast and main sections of the park.*

Hawaii **185**

# . . . volcanoes

*A TOE OF LAVA from a new flow cools atop an older flow where plant life has begun. Ferns and lichen appear early on lava flows. Where rainfall is light, lava remains almost bare for years. Ropy lava (below) is pahoehoe; rough, cindery kind is aa.*

DAVID MUENCH

DAVID MUENCH

*A STEAMING HALEMAUMAU, viewed here across the scarred floor of Kilauea crater, is less frightening than the fiery Halemaumau in the photograph on the previous page.*

Hawaii **187**

DAVID MUENCH

. . . volcanoes

NORMAN A. PLATE

BILL GLEASNER

*A LIFELESS LANDSCAPE borders the Devastation
Trail (left), a half-mile-long boardwalk that
crosses a deep carpet of pumice through a skeleton
forest of dead ohia trees. A 1959 eruption in
Kilauea Iki (Little Kilauea) rained cinders on this
region. Thurston Lava Tube (above) was formed when
the outer crust of a lava flow hardened while the
molten river of lava within continued to move.
Early Hawaiians used similar tubes as burial caves.*

Hawaii **189**

*ON A WINDSWEPT PLATEAU, backed by the green Kohala Mountains, Parker Ranch lands cover 325,000 acres of the Big Island. Cattle were first introduced in the Islands in 1793, when Captain Vancouver presented a small herd to Kamehameha. Today 70,000 head roam Parker Ranch. They are shipped to Honolulu markets from Kawaihae Harbor—as they were when the above photograph was taken in the early 1890s—but methods of transport are different. In early days, cattle were hoisted individually onto interisland steamers; now trailer trucks filled with cattle are shipped by barge.*

**190** Hawaii

# Kohala is a region of contrasts

# . . . Kohala

*WELL-PRESERVED Imiola Church in Waimea was built in 1857 by missionary Lorenzo Lyons. An energetic and well-loved preacher, Reverend Lyons composed many Hawaiian hymns still sung today. New England-style on the outside, the little church is Hawaiian in feeling inside, with walls paneled in koa and chandeliers made of koa bowls.*

*BACKED BY GENTLE HILLS, the trim, well-cared-for buildings of Waimea are scattered about the cool, pastoral plateau that is part of bustling Parker Ranch. Waimea has a new shopping center and new homes, but it still has gingerbread houses, colorful flower gardens, and white picket fences.*

Hawaii **193**

# . . . Kohala

TOM TRACY

*REMOTE VALLEYS AND SUNNY BEACHES contrast in Kohala. Beautiful valleys, laced with waterfalls and resplendent with native plants, cut the windward face of the mile-high Kohala Mountains. On the opposite page, three hikers (barely visible at right of waterfall) follow a trail behind Kapoloa Falls in Pololu Valley. On the leeward side of the mountains, the lavishly landscaped terraces and golf fairways of the Mauna Kea Beach Hotel spread over the slopes above a curve of sandy beach fronting Kaunaoa Bay (above).*

Hawaii **195**

# The Kona Coast...
# modern resorts and
# old Hawaii

*A PALACE and the oldest church in the Islands lie just a few steps apart along Kailua's waterfront (opposite page). Gracious, verandahed Hulihee Palace, built in 1837-38 by Hawaii's governor, Kuakini, served as King Kalakaua's summer palace in the 1880s. Behind it is Mokuaikaua Church, built in 1837 by the first missionaries. The same buildings dominated the scene on boat day in about 1885 (above). In the early 1900s, a lone automobile appeared on the road bordering Kailua Bay (left).*

Hawaii **197**

# . . . the Kona Coast

*A LOVE OF FISHING seems to be an Island characteristic. Kailua's waterfront (left) is a popular gathering place where fishermen of all ages try their luck, usually with ample advice from passersby. Keauhou Bay (above), a long-time anchorage and canoe landing for Kona fishermen, is a growing resort area now, but local families still find its pier a productive fishing spot.*

DAVID CORNWELL

*ONLY COFFEE INDUSTRY in the nation thrives in the cool uphill section of Kona, where plants are shaded by a dependable afternoon cloud cover and nourished by rich volcanic soil. Most beans are dried mechanically today, but at Kona's largest mill, some are still sun-dried in this large shed with a rollaway roof.*

**200** Hawaii

# . . . the Kona Coast

*COFFEE "CHERRIES" ripen unevenly on the stem, and each berry must be picked at exactly the right moment. Picking and sorting were done by hand in the early 1900s. Mechanical pickers, which shake the ripe berries from the plant, are in use now, but on small family farms, youngsters often help with the picking. Once grown on all the major islands, coffee is grown commercially today only on Hawaii's Kona Coast.*

# . . . the Kona Coast

A MUCH-PHOTOGRAPHED LANDMARK, tiny blue-and-white St. Peter's Catholic Church occupies a picturesque site among palm trees at the edge of Kahaluu Bay.

*PERCHED ON A HILLSIDE near Honaunau, St. Benedict's Church has a charming carpenter's Gothic exterior. Inside decorations, done by Belgian priest John Berchmans Velghe about 1900, are the reason for its nickname, the "Painted Church."*

*A FOLK ART MASTERPIECE, the interior of the Painted Church is decorated with Hawaiian motifs and copies of religious works. On the wall behind the altar, a perspective painting gives the illusion that the vaulted nave continues.*

Hawaii **203**

. . . the Kona Coast

*A HAVEN for defeated warriors, noncombatants, and lawbreakers for 400 years, the City of Refuge at Honaunau was the highest ranking of the refuges that once stood in every major district of the Islands. The thatch structure on the point (left) is a reconstruction of Hale-o-Keawe, which became the main temple after 1650. Lava boulders fitted together without mortar formed the Great Wall (top of page). Wooden figures (above) are replicas of refuge gods.*

PHOTOGRAPHS BY TOM TRACY (LEFT, ABOVE RIGHT), ELLS MARUGG (ABOVE LEFT)

Hawaii **205**

*A LONE OHIA tree thrusts up from the lava wasteland on Mauna Loa's slope. The Saddle Road crosses the island over a windswept, lava-blanketed pass between Mauna Loa and Mauna Kea, the two highest peaks in the Hawaiian archipelago.*

# Atop the highest mountains

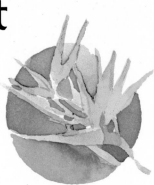

A MANTLE OF SNOW blankets Mauna Loa around observatories
where scientists conduct astronomical studies in clear air
far removed from population centers. Skiers find runs from
1,000 yards to 3 miles long on slopes that are usually
snow-covered from December to May.

BOONE MORRISON

DAVID MUENCH

Hawaii **207**

# Index